SCHWEITZER'S PSYCHOANALYSIS OF JESUS CHRIST

& Other Essays in Christian Psychotherapy

SCHWEITZER'S PSYCHOANALYSIS OF JESUS CHRIST

& Other Essays in Christian Psychotherapy

—

JOHN WARWICK MONTGOMERY
Foreword by Archie Johnson

Schweitzer's Psychoanalysis of Jesus Christ and Other Essays in Christian Psychotherapy

© 2023 New Reformation Publications

Published by:
1517 Publishing
PO Box 54032
Irvine, CA 92619-4032

Publisher's Cataloging-In-Publication Data
(Prepared by The Donohue Group, Inc.)

Names: Montgomery, John Warwick, author. | Johnson, Archie, Dr., writer of foreword.
Title: Schweitzer's psychoanalysis of Jesus Christ : and other essays in Christian psychotherapy / John Warwick Montgomery ; foreword by Archie Johnson.
Description: Irvine, CA : 1517 Publishing, [2023] | Includes bibliographical references.
Identifiers: ISBN: 978-1-956658-63-7 (hardcover) | 978-1-956658-64-4 (paperback) | 978-1-956658-65-1 (ebook)
Subjects: LCSH: Psychotherapy—Religious aspects—Christianity. | Psychoanalysis—Religious aspects—Christianity. | Psychology, Religious. | Jesus Christ—Psychology. | Schweitzer, Albert, 1875-1965—Criticism and interpretation. | Apologetics. | BISAC: RELIGION / Psychology of Religion. | RELIGION / Christian Theology / Apologetics. | RELIGION / Christian Theology / History.
Classification: LCC: BV4012 .M66 2023 | DDC: 261.515—dc23

To my dear wife

CAROL
the best of therapists

Contents

Introductory quotation

—Vous croyez que Van Gogh aurait coupé son oreille s'il avait été psychanalysé ?

—Certainement si, mais il aurait su pourquoi.

[—Do you think Van Gogh would have cut off his ear if he had been psychoanalyzed?]

[—Very definitely. But he would have known why.]

André Sauret, *Complexes* ;
préface Pierre Mac Orlan
(Monte Carlo : Éditions du Livre « La Ruche » 1948).
Copy 850 of 890 numbered copies.

Foreword

My Tribute to Dr. John W. Montgomery

Late one evening, I received an email from Professor Montgomery. He wrote, "Dear Archie, you will be staggered to learn that I have received a university Diploma in psychoanalysis, and I have completed a short book of essays on the subject." I was stunned! I sat down to process his exciting news. He asked me to endorse this book! I was elated!

For the readers of Montgomery's new book, I want to provide a brief note of appreciation that expresses how important Dr. Montgomery has been in my personal and professional life.

I initially met Dr. Montgomery in San Diego at the International Congress on Biblical Inerrancy. I was completing my undergraduate degree in philosophy. I was enthralled by how many theological booths were at the Congress. I was surprised that very few attendees were waiting to greet some of the top Christian scholars at the Convention.

Then Montgomery appeared, and crowds of people surrounded the legal and apologetic rock star. After hearing his lecture, I decided to train with him, one of the top legal and apologetic minds of my lifetime. I have never regretted my choice.

When I returned home, my friends said that if I studied philosophy, I would no longer be a Christian. Therefore, I took that as a challenge. Before meeting Professor Montgomery in California, I discovered his extensive writings in a bibliography given to me ironically by our top atheist professor in philosophy. I was more determined to finish my degree in two years so that I could train with Montgomery in California.

At that point, before ever meeting Montgomery, I read all of his books. I then decided to meet with my professors, who were openly critical of Christianity. These were science, philosophy, mathematics, political science, religion, and history professors. I offered each one of them Montgomery's books to read before we met.

I used the starter text, Montgomery's *History and Christianity (now History, Law, and Christianity).*

I would then cross-examine my professors, in a Montgomery-like fashion, based on their readings. After many intense discussions, much to my surprise, these professors never openly criticized Christianity again. The Montgomery maxim: the only reason anyone should be a Christian is because it's true.

I spoke to Dr. Francis Schaeffer earlier at the Congress in San Diego. He encouraged me to study with Montgomery. Upon graduation, I was determined to attend law school under Dr. Montgomery in California and Strasbourg.

It was only fitting that our law school later awarded Francis Schaeffer the honorary Doctor of Laws in Strasbourg, France. I suddenly realized that I had made a full circle in my advanced training with Professor Montgomery.

Dr. Montgomery's latest book is a tour de force. He beautifully highlights how modern psychiatric treatment is mindless—it has lost its mind! Contemporary forms of psychotherapy are, *Soulless*—psychological and spiritual problems require a transcendent solution, as Montgomery nicely documents. No, citing Freud, Jung, or Albert Schweitzer in his flawed diagnosis of Jesus will never be the same as quoting Holy Scripture. Unfortunately, the modern church has also lost its revelational understanding of the complex dynamics of the Soul.

In contrast, as Montgomery richly documents, contemporary psychiatric (and psychoanalytic) treatment has lost its mind/brain. Dr. Montgomery's latest book is a fresh movement of the Spirit of God to a lost and dying world without Christ. The answer: Put Christianity back into the discussion of what is genuine treatment, and Montgomery's newest book wonderfully points us in that direction.

In my most recent conversation with Professor Montgomery, he said, "Archie, you have done very well for yourself!" I responded, "Dr. Montgomery, you have been my inspiration!" What a tremendous honor, Dr. Montgomery, to introduce your book. As C.S. Lewis said about one of your earlier writings, and I concur regarding this new installment, "It could not be better!"

Thank you, Dr. Montgomery!

Archie Johnson, Ph.D., LLM
Senior Clinical Director
International Clinical Fellow in Neuroscience and Clinical Psychoanalysis

Author of *The Talking Cure*, the upcoming: *The Christian Cure; How Does Christianity Cure?* and the two-volume *Christian Jurisprudence, and The Theological Cure.*

Chapter One

Personal Perspective

Fundamental to successful therapeutic practice is self-understanding on the part of the therapist. For this reason, personal psychotherapy is generally expected or required of the novice practitioner. Therefore, the critiques in this section of the book are preceded by a brief description of the writer's background. The advantages of such an approach are: (1) to understand why the writer has chosen his particular areas of critique, (2) to appreciate his critiques against the background of his particular concerns, and (3) to minimize what is generally (unfortunate) *ad hominem* argumentation.

I was born in a small town in upstate western New York State. My father was a merchant in the coal and feed business, and my mother a former schoolteacher. My father did not do well academically; my mother was the first person in her family to receive a University degree (from Cornell University). They both attended a liberal community church. I spent most of my childhood living with my maternal grandmother, a Baptist fundamentalist. I excelled in school, graduating valedictorian of my class. I had intended to study engineering at the Rensselaer Polytechnic Institute but changed direction at the last minute because of the narrowness of the curriculum and instead enrolled in liberal arts at Cornell.

Early in my freshman year, I met a third-year engineering student who introduced me to classic, biblical Christianity. My objections to the faith melted in the face of major contemporary writings of an apologetic nature (C. S. Lewis, Edward John Carnell, Wilbur Smith). After graduating with double majors in philosophy and the classics (Greco-Roman language and literature), I took graduate work in library science, served as a reference librarian at the University of California, Berkeley, and ultimately received the Ph.D. at the Graduate Library School of the University of Chicago.

Finding a librarian's career rather non-fulfilling, I accepted an appointment as chair of the history department at the then Waterloo Lutheran University, some sixty miles west of Toronto, Canada. A Canada Council post-doctoral research fellowship made obtaining a second doctorate at the University of Strasbourg, France, possible. By then, I had two small children by my first marriage to my childhood sweetheart.

I returned from France to a professorship at an evangelical Protestant theological seminary in the Chicago suburbs. Various national debates with atheists and religious modernists ensued. I commenced the study of law, owing to its positive value in the defense of historic Christian faith, and ultimately founded a Christian law school in California and served as its dean for six years.

My marriage deteriorated into a divorce. I remarried, successfully competed for a senior lectureship in law at the University of Bedfordshire, England, and was ultimately elevated to professorial rank. Meanwhile, I obtained the higher doctorate in law at Cardiff University, Wales.

On retirement from the University of Bedfordshire, I moved to France, where, as an English barrister and Paris *avocat,* I successfully argued religious liberty cases before the European Court of Human Rights in Strasbourg. My second wife passed away after an unsuccessful operation, and I married a Canadian who had been a former student of mine.

The preceding autobiographical description will explain why my following critiques stress *epistemology* (the branch of philosophy dealing with truth issues), *semantics* (language as related to truth), and *theology/religion.*[1]

---

[1]   For more biographical detail, see J. W. Montgomery, *Fighting the Good Fight* (3rd ed.; Bonn, Germany: Verlag fuer Kultur und Wissenschaft, 2022).

Chapter Two

Schweitzer's Psychoanalytic Evaluation of Jesus

Schweitzer's Life and Theology

Albert Schweitzer (1875-1965) was one of the most famous international figures of the 20th century. He was lauded particularly as a humanitarian doctor, treating natives in the hospital he founded at Lambaréné (then in French Equatorial Africa, now the Republic of Gabon). In 1952, Schweitzer received the Nobel Peace Prize for his labors.

It is said that Louella Parsons touted Schweitzer as "the greatest man who ever lived." (A comedic 33 1/3 vinyl has Parsons arriving at the Lambaréné hospital to visit Schweitzer. On being informed of her visit, Schweitzer said, "Have the crocodiles been fed this morning?")

Schweitzer was renowned in three fields: theology, music, and medical humanitarianism.

His theological fame stemmed from his book. *The Quest of the Historical Jesus* (1906). During the 18th and 19th centuries, "historical biographies" of Jesus were produced that presented Jesus as the ideal human, a kind of apex of the evolutionary process. Schweitzer's *Quest* argued, in diametric contrast, that the historical Jesus saw himself as an apocalyptic prophet whose task was to bring in the ultimate divine kingdom.

> The Baptist appears, and cries: "Repent, for the Kingdom of Heaven is at hand." Soon after that comes Jesus, and in the knowledge that He is the coming Son of Man lays hold of the wheel of the world to set it moving on that last revolution which is to bring all ordinary history to a close. It refuses to turn, and He throws Himself upon it. Then it does turn; and crushes Him. Instead of bringing in the eschatological conditions, He has destroyed them. The wheel rolls onward, and the mangled body of the one immeasurably great Man, who was strong enough to think of Himself as the spiritual ruler of mankind and to bend history to

His purpose, is hanging upon it still. That is His victory and His reign.[1]

Tom (N. T.) Wright has attempted, without much success, to put a positive spin on this sentiment:

Albert Schweitzer, a century or more ago, used another strong image. Jesus, he said, was like a man convinced the wheel of history was going to turn in the opposite direction. He waited for this to happen, but it didn't. Then he threw himself upon the wheel, and it crushed him – but it did indeed start to turn in the other direction.

Schweitzer did not, in fact, believe in the New Testament gospel. Rather, he sees Jesus as an unknown, undefinable object of personal identification, perhaps not unlike the Jesus of Dietrich Bonhoeffer's final theological stage: "the place to be." Listen to Schweitzer's characterization of Jesus:

He comes to us as one unknown, nameless, just as in an ancient time, by the lakeside, he came to

---

[1] Schweitzer, *The Quest of the Historical Jesus*, trans. W. Montgomery (2nd ed.; London: Adam and Charles Black, 1911). pp. 368-69. Subsequent editions do not appear to contain the quoted paragraph; that is the case with the "first complete edition," edited by John Bowden (London: SCM Press, 2000).

those men who knew him not. He speaks the same word to us: "Follow me!" He places us at the tasks which he must fulfill in our time. To those who obey him, wise or simple, he will reveal Himself in the labors, conflicts, and miseries they will experience in communion with him. As an ineffable mystery, they shall come inwardly to know who he is.[2]

Shortly before his death, Schweitzer became a life member of the Unitarian Universalist Church of the Larger Fellowship. Of the Trinity, he asked rhetorically, "Did Christ or Saint Paul believe in it?"[3]

Understandably, though Schweitzer had the greatest admiration for Bach's music, his

---

[2] Schweitzer, "The Unknown One," in his Pilgrimage to Humanity, trans. Walter E. Stuermann (New York: Philosophical Library, 1961), p. 85. This is the concluding paragraph in all of the editions of Schweitzer's Quest of the Historical Jesus.

[3] It is strange that Schweitzer did not recall Jesus' Great Commission, with which the Gospel of Matthew ends (28:16-20): "Go ye therefore, and teach all nations, baptizing them in the name of the Father, and of the Son, and of the Holy Ghost: teaching them to observe all things whatsoever I have commanded you: and, lo, I am with you always, even unto the end of the world." Here, Jesus' assertion of the Trinitarian nature of God could not be clearer: baptize in ONE name, represented by THREE PERSONS (Father, Son, and Holy Spirit).

two-volume work on the composer[4] shows no understanding of or appreciation for the central position Luther's Trinitarian and Christ-centered theology had in Bach's life and musical career.[5]

More important in many ways to Schweitzer than traditional Christian belief was his commitment to "reverence for life." Though this connects well with current environmentalist emphases both within the church and without, it also has its dark side. Medical and lay visitors to Lambaréné reported their concerns over Schweitzer's reticence to kill even insects within the hospital.

Schweitzer's Psychoanalysis of Jesus

Albert Schweitzer became a simple physician, not a psychiatrist. But, unlike medical schools in England, where physicians receive "Bachelor of Medicine" degrees on graduation (logically, since they are taking just a first degree in medicine), or in the United States, where the M.D. degree requires no graduate

---

[4] Schweitzer, J. S. Bach, trans. Ernest Newman, preface C. M. Widor (2 vols.; London: Macmillan, 1950).

[5] See Schweitzer, "Johann Sebastian Bach," in his Pilgrimage to Humanity (op. cit.), pp. 64-72.

thesis at all, graduation from a German or French medical school requires, as with the Ph.D., the production and defense of a scholarly dissertation. The degree is thus a genuine academic doctorate, not a professional doctorate (U.S.) or a mere courtesy title (the United Kingdom).

Schweitzer chose as his thesis title, *The Psychiatric Study of Jesus: Exposition and Criticism,* which was successfully defended in 1911 and first published in 1913.[6]

The background of this choice was the existence, in Schweitzer's time, of certain medical treatises that purported to show Jesus as mentally ill. Schweitzer's short dissertation was an effort to counteract such views.

The following extracts from the thesis will give the reader a taste of Schweitzer's argumentative approach:[7]

> The recorded hallucinations of Jesus, according to Binet-Sanglé, cannot have been the only ones, as

---

[6] Schweitzer, The Psychiatric Study of Jesus: Exposition and Criticism, trans. Charles R. Joy, foreword Winfred Overholser (Boston: Beacon Press, 1948). Appropriately, the English translation of Schweitzer's doctoral thesis was put into circulation by the foremost American Unitarian publishing house.

[7] *Ibid.,* pp. 44, 57.

insane mystics almost always suffer from hallucinations of muscle-sense. "In later periods," he goes on, "come the secondary psychomotor symptoms, constituting a kind of theomanic possession." He cites as examples of sensory hallucinations the places in the four Gospels in which Jesus says that the Father speaks through him but concedes that they cannot be defined specifically.

Before we begin the discussion of the picture of psychosis drawn by the three authors, attention should be called to the fact that the assertion that this is a question of acquired mental disease has already *a priori* very little probability about it. Binet-Sanglé cites a large number of clinical observations of sick people who have suffered from religious paranoia accompanied by all kinds of hallucinations and also points out the frequency with which these cases, so familiar to every psychiatrist, occur. He forgets, however, that cases of "chronic delirium in its systematic development," which resemble the paranoiac form of Kraepelin's *Dementia praecox*, are for the most part hospitalized soon after the onset of their illness, and that these forms of mental disease are exactly the type which do not win supporters and disciples and found sects. The numerous hallucinations, the catatonic symptoms in the broadest sense of the word (autism), and the effects of dissociation make these sick people incapable of consecutive activity; if some renunciation of activity takes place it seldom corresponds to the delusional contents of a consciousness which has been impaired by psychosis, The fact is well known that sick people suffering from delusions of persecution, particularly from a morbid fear of physical persecution, continue to carry on their work years on end and extremely seldom draw the practical conclusion from their hallucinations and delusions, namely that they should defend themselves against their persecutors—either legally or illegally; if in some fleeting mood they do this, it happens because of some state of excitement, and not, therefore, because of conscious and logical inferences. The persecuted psychotics, who are actually and continually on the defensive, the "persecuted persecutors" of the French, belong to the group of congenital psychopaths and do not suffer from an acquired mental disease.

Here is Schweitzer's concluding summary:[8]

The criticism of the psychopathological writings which we are considering yields, then, the following results:

1. The material which is in agreement with these books is for the most part unhistorical.

---

[8] *Ibid.* p. 72

2. Out of the material which is certainly historical, a number of acts and utterances of Jesus impress the authors as pathological because the latter are too little/acquainted with the contemporary thought of the time to be able to do justice to it. A series of wrong deductions springs also from the fact that they have not the least understanding of the peculiar problems inherent in the course of the public ministry.

3. From these false preconceptions and with the help of entirely hypothetical symptoms, they construct pictures of sickness which are themselves artifacts and which, moreover, cannot be made to conform exactly with the clinical forms of sickness diagnosed by the authors.

4. The only symptoms to be accepted as historical and possibly to be discussed from the psychiatric point of view—the high estimate which Jesus has of himself and perhaps also the hallucination at the baptism—fall far short of proving the existence of mental illness.

Was Schweitzer's psychiatric defense of Jesus successful?

The thesis received high praise from early reviewers. Here is an example from a University of Chicago publication, which, notably, points out that Schweitzer used only the Synoptic Gospels as his source for biographical information on Jesus since he considered the Gospel of John as unreliable historically:[9]

> He insists, in the first place, that anyone who makes such claims must base them on the facts of the case history. Apart from the unreliability of historical facts in general, this means that in analysing the mental state of Jesus, we must limit ourselves to those parts of the gospels accepted by scholarship as historical. This clearly rules out the gospel of John, from which most of the supposed evidence of paranoia had been cited. Secondly, Schweitzer points out that no man lives in a vacuum. The common beliefs of the people of Jesus' generation, race, and religion—in particular, beliefs in the imminent advent of the Messiah, the coming of the Kingdom on earth, and the angels—can in no way be regarded as symptoms of mental aberration in him. Again, the occurrence of hallucinations is not confined to the mentally ill.

The Foreword to the English translation of the German dissertation was provided by the then-president of the American Psychiatric Association,

---

[9] Bentley Glass, in *3 Yearbook of Psychoanalysis* 401 (1947).

one Wilfred Overholser. Overholser was not entirely convinced by Schweitzer's argument. A portion of his evaluation of Schweitzer's work deserves quoting here:

> Since the authors discussed by Dr. Schweitzer agree on one point, namely that Jesus suffered from some form of "paranoia," a few words concerning this type of mental disorder may not be out of place. The word is an old one—it was used in the Hippocratic writings, though in a general sense, as meaning mental disease. It was introduced into German psychiatry as early as 1818 by Heinroth, but with so loose a definition that at one time from 70 to 80 percent of the patients in European mental hospitals were diagnosed as suffering from "paranoia." Indeed, as late as 1887 a French psychiatrist (Séglas) referred to it as a word which had "la signification la plus vaste et la plus mal définie." Gradually it came to include a variety of clinical groups characterized by ideas of persecution and grandeur, in varying proportions. Some of these groups exhibited almost entirely a distortion and misinterpretation of actual facts, others some elaboration with fabrication, while some showed such a loss of contact with reality as to cause the patient to suffer from hallucinations in one or more of the sensory spheres. A religious coloring of the delusions

is far from uncommon. Kraepelin, the great German descriptive psychiatrist, defined these various groups—paranoia, paraphrenia (now generally referred to as paranoid condition) and dementia praecox of the paranoid type, his final formulation appearing about 1913. To Kraepelin and his school, as to the French school of psychiatry, paranoia was largely a question of constitution; it was based on the makeup of the person, developed insidiously and progressively, and was essentially unamenable to treatment. They looked on it as almost if not quite entirely a disturbance of the intellectual functions. It was only in 1906 that Bleuler emphasized the importance in the disorder of reaction to life situations, as opposed to a fatalistic interpretation, and it was after the appearance of Schweitzer's answer to the psychiatrists that a more dynamic interpretation of the mechanisms of paranoia and the paranoid conditions came about as a result of Freud's penetrating observations

One must have a good case history. In the case of Jesus, we have virtually none. The first Gospels were probably written 40 or more years after the death of Jesus; as such, their accuracy as to detail, at least as psychiatric documents, must be questioned. Furthermore, we know nothing except by tradition of any but the last year or so (at the most) of Jesus' life, and in all accounts there is a gap of at least 18 years. We know very little of his relations with his mother and siblings and, while we know something of the multifarious social, religious and economic influences of the time, we know very little of the manner in which they played upon him and moulded his feelings and reactions. The perils of diagnosis *à distance* are great![10]

But the problem with Schweitzer's attempt, on cultural/sociological grounds, to justify psychiatrically Jesus' misconception of who he really was goes far deeper than "diagnosis at a distance," as we shall see.

Since Schweitzer's time, much new work has been done in the psychiatric realm in regard to "delusion." Here is a current definition and summary of some of the most common delusional types:[11]

A delusion is a belief that is clearly false and that indicates an abnormality in the affected person's content of thought. The false belief is not accounted for by the person's cultural or religious background or his or her level of intelligence. The

---

[10] Overholser, in Schweitzer, op. cit., pp. 13-14.

[11] Chandra Kiran and S. Chaudhury, "Understanding Delusions," 18/1 Industrial Psychiatry J. 3-18 (Jan.-Jun., 2009).

key feature of a delusion is the degree to which the person is convinced that the belief is true. A person with a delusion will hold firmly to the belief regardless of evidence to the contrary. Delusions can be difficult to distinguish from overvalued ideas, which are unreasonable ideas that a person holds, but the affected person has at least some level of doubt as to its truthfulness. A person with a delusion is absolutely convinced that the delusion is real. Delusions are a symptom of either a medical, neurological, or mental disorder. Delusions may be present in any of the following mental disorders: (1) Psychotic disorders, or disorders in which the affected person has a diminished or distorted sense of reality and cannot distinguish the real from the unreal, including schizophrenia, schizoaffective disorder, delusional disorder, schizophreniform disorder, shared psychotic disorder, brief psychotic disorder, and substance-induced psychotic disorder, (2) Bipolar disorder, (3) Major depressive disorder with psychotic features (4) Delirium, and (5) Dementia.

[Common Delusional Types:]

Delusion of persecution

It is the most frequent content of delusion. It was distinguished from other types of delusion and other forms of melancholia by Lasegue (1852). The interfering agent may be animate or inanimate, other people or machines; may be systems, organizations, or institutions rather than individuals. Sometimes the patient experiences persecution as a vague influence without knowing who is responsible. May occur in conditions like: Schizophrenia, Affective psychosis: Manic, Depressive type, and Organic states: Acute, chronic. Persecutory overvalued ideas are a prominent facet of the litiginous type of paranoid personality disorder.

Grandiose delusions

In this the patient may believe himself to be a famous celebrity or to have supernatural powers. Expansive or grandiose delusional beliefs may extend to objects, so leading to delusion of invention. Grandiose and expansive delusions may also be part of fantastic hallucinosis, in which all forms of hallucinations occur.

Religious delusions

The religious nature of the delusion is seen as a disorder of content dependent on the patient's social background, interests and peer group. The form of the delusion is dictated by the nature of the illness. So religious delusions are not caused by excessive religious belief, nor by the wrongdoing which the patient attributes as cause, but they simply accentuate that when a person becomes mentally ill his delusions reflect, in their content, his predominant interests and concerns. Although common, they formed a higher proportion in the nineteenth century than in the twentieth century and are still prevalent in developing countries.

Delusions of guilt and unworthiness

Initially the patient may be self-reproachful and self-critical which may ultimately lead to delusions of guilt and unworthiness, when the patients believe that they are bad or evil persons and have ruined their family. They may claim to have committed an unpardonable sin and insist that they will rot in hell for this. These are common in depressive illness, and may lead to suicide or homicide.

Delusions of negation/nihilistic delusions

These are the reverse of grandiose delusions where oneself, objects or situations are expansive and enriched; there is also a perverse grandiosity about the nihilistic delusions themselves. Feelings of guilt and hypochondriacal ideas are developed to their most extreme, depressive form in nihilistic delusions.

To be sure, the question is whether any of these delusions would apply to Jesus. The only serious candidates would appear to be religious delusions and delusions of the grandiose sort. But the ministry of Jesus surely belies any grandiosity on Jesus' part. (He often stressed that the Kingdom was open only to those who entered it as little children, and the Parable of the Pharisee and the tax collector in Luke 18 could not make His condemnation of pride and moral self-satisfaction plainer.) As for religious delusion, there is no doubt that Jesus, again and again, made divine claims for Himself. But the issue here is simply whether those claims of Jesus concerning Himself were, or were not, *true.*

If the key to genuine mental health is accurate self-knowledge, and if Jesus, being only a human prophet (as Schweitzer believed), was convinced that he was the Messiah, slated to bring the present age to its apocalyptic end, then a large question mark would seem to fall over the claim that he was not indeed paranoic. His sanity would surely deserve psychiatric examination.

Moreover, against the views of the Jewish religious establishment of his time, Jesus' view of himself far transcended Schweitzer's limited, humanistic picture: Jesus claimed to be no less than God Almighty, come to earth to save humanity from their sins.

This picture of Jesus is anything but that of an apocalyptic Jewish boy scout helping little old ladies to cross the Sea of Galilee, and it is present both in the Synoptic Gospels (which Schweitzer evidently considered worthy of factual acceptance) and the Gospel of John (which he did not).

Mark, generally considered to be the earliest of the four Gospels, begins with Jesus miraculously healing a paralytic by forgiving his sins, eliciting the comment from those present, "Who can forgive sins but God only?" (Mark 2). Matthew's Gospel (26:63-65) records the condemnation of Jesus for blasphemy, which demonstrates that Jesus' enemies were perfectly convinced that He made no less than divine claims.

The author of the Gospel of John was patently the Apostle of that name, as is supported by his connection with John's disciple Papias;[12] it follows that

---

[12] See Montgomery, "The Fourth Gospel Yesterday and Today," in his *The Suicide of Christian Theology* (Minneapolis: Bethany Fellowship, 1971), pp. 428-65. "It has been thought either that [Irenaeus] was confused about which John Polycarp referred to, or that he deliberately concocted the story of Polycarp's relationship with John in order to forge a link between himself and an apostle. Many have held that Irenaeus' memory of a childhood

John's account of Jesus' earthly ministry is as valuable a source for Jesus' view of Himself as are the three Synoptic Gospels. In the Fourth Gospel, Jesus asserts that "before Abraham was, I am" (8:58)—an incontrovertible claim to divine existence. In John 14:6, Jesus declares: "I am the way, the truth, and the life: no one comes to the Father but by me"; later in that same chapter, Jesus accepts Philip's declaration that He, Jesus, is indeed, "My Lord and my God."

There is the story of the theological seminary student who was assigned to pastoral work at a hospital for psychotics. On entering a ward, he met a gentleman wearing a tricorne and speaking French. "And who are you?" asked the seminarian politely.

---

acquaintance with Polycarp, though perhaps vivid, was faulty at this point, or perhaps that he never understood that the John about whom Polycarp reminisced was not the apostle but John the Elder, mentioned (apparently) by Papias (Eusebius, *HE* 3.39.4). This theory at least, I think, may now be laid to rest... Irenaeus' testimony, that Polycarp was one of a number of Asian leaders who learned from the apostle John, and even from others known as apostles, has the support of considerable circumstantial evidence and certainly faces no disqualifying counter evidence." (Charles E. Hill, *From the Lost Teaching of Polycarp* (MohrSiebeck, 2006), pp.173,177). "The elder [John] was the Apostle John. That John the elder and apostle makes the Apostle Peter the source of Mark's material and ascribes the First Gospel to the Apostle Matthew." R. H. Gundry, *The Old Is Better* (MohrSiebeck, 2005/Wipf & Stock, 2010), p.68.

Answer: "*Napoléon, bien sûr,*" "And what makes you think that?" countered the pastoral intern. Reply: "*Parce que Dieu me l'a dit*" [God told me]. A voice was then heard across the room: "I DID NOT!"

As any psychoanalytic or clinical psychiatrist worthy of the title would surely agree, thinking you are God—IF YOU ARE NOT GOD—is patent evidence of mental aberration.

Of course, the one Person who could make such a claim and remain mentally sound would be God Himself. Had Schweitzer accepted the full picture of the historical Jesus found in the eyewitness New Testament records, he could have made a successful argument, *but not otherwise.*

And why did Schweitzer not accept those claims? For the very same reason that he sidestepped the fulfillment of Old Testament prophecy in Jesus' earthly career and paid no attention to His miracles or the facticity of His resurrection from the dead: while rejecting the 18th-19th century evolutionistic portrait of Jesus, Schweitzer accepted the so-called "assured results of biblical criticism" that were just as much the product of secular, anti-miraculous scientism as the non-apocalyptic portrait of Jesus characteristic of the theological

modernism of the time.[13] Schweitzer apparently
never took the trouble to read the devastating ref-
utations of the higher criticism of his day (e.g.,
F. C. Baur and the so-called Tübingen school) produced by such stellar scholars as archeologist Sir
William Ramsay, nor does he show any acquaintance with B. B. Warfield's classic, *The Lord of
Glory: A Study of the Designations of Our Lord in
the New Testament with Especial Reference to His
Deity* (1907).[14]

Therefore, our conclusion must be to thank
Schweitzer for ridding us of evolutionary Jesuses,
but to reject his alternative. Jesus was simply who he
said he was, and therefore free of all self-deception
or mental aberration. As he indubitably claimed,
he was the Messianic fulfilment of biblical revelation, the God who loved us so much that, even

---

[13] Owing to similar acceptance of rationalistic biblical criticism,
the later, post-Bultmannian, so-called "new quest" of the historical
Jesus (Günter Bornkamm. Fuchs, Conzelmann, Käsemann, James
M. Robinson, *et al.*) has had no more success than Schweitzer's
humanistic, eschatological portrait. On this, see Montgomery,
Crisis in Lutheran Theology (rev. ed.; Irvine, CA: New Reformation
Publications, 2022), 3 vols.

[14] Today, the historical soundness of the New Testament picture
of Christ has been confirmed by, *inter alia*, Richard Bauckham,
The Gospels As Eyewitness Testimony (2nd ed.; Grand Rapids, MI:
Eerdmans, 2017).

though a fallen race caused His death, he sacrificed Himself to save everyone who believes in His salvatory work.[15]

Appendix: Albert Schweitzer Redivivus

A few words (more would be superfluous) concerning a new book psychologizing Jesus: *The Historical Christ: A Cognitive Psychologist's Perspective,* by Bruce W. Behrman, emeritus professor at California State University, Sacramento (Wipf and Stock, 2023).

The book's title is a gross misnomer since the Christ analyzed has virtually nothing to do with the Christ of history. Remarkably, despite the failure of Schweitzer's psychological treatment of Jesus, more than a century later, we are given a parallel analysis, incorporating the same errors. Could this be due, at least in part, to the fact that neither of the two authors had scientific training beyond that of a general physician (Schweitzer) or an academic psychologist (Behrman)?

---

[15] See also, Montgomery, "Schweitzer, Albert," in: *Encyclopedia of Christian Civilization,* ed. G. T. Kurian (Oxford: Blackwell, 2011).

Behrman's thesis is that Jesus suffered from manic-depressive illness, but, as with not a few talented, creative, artistic greats (Byron, Tennyson, Van Gogh, among others), this did not prevent him from mighty accomplishments.

Evidence of Jesus' manic depression? Extreme mood changes and great compassion toward others—characteristics that often accompany such a psychosis. But, most telling, *Jesus actually identified himself with God!*

Behrman's key argument, like Schweitzer's, is that Jesus made divine claims. But, unlike Schweitzer, who rejected John's Gospel as lacking historical value, Behrman asserts "the primacy of John" in demonstrating Jesus' manic depression (pp. 130 ff.).

> I view the Gospel of John as the primary source for assessing the life of Jesus. I say this primarily because of the manic depression hypothesis.... Jesus did imagine that he was God and said so. He likely asserted that he was sent from God but just as often said he was God. This assertion of divinity is not uncommon among manic depressive patients.... Jesus felt he was God incarnate, best expressed by the 'I am' sayings recorded in John. However, identification with God would have constituted a

terrifying blasphemy. These disparate feelings, the sense of identity with God and its attendant guilt, would have produced a severe crisis of identity in Jesus.

How could Jesus not have been suffering from mental illness when he made such claims? We have provided a detailed answer in our examination of Schweitzer's argument. We do not deny that to consider yourself as God equals a lack of self-knowledge and a strong dose of paranoic mania—*on condition, however, and solely on condition, that one is in fact NOT God.* Both Behrman and Schweitzer dismiss the solid, contemporary, documentary evidence that Jesus fulfilled innumerable Old Testament prophecies and performed innumerable miraculous acts, culminating in his resurrection from the dead. This historical evidence fully supports his claim to be a Deity and belies all psychological efforts to explain it away. If Behrman's book were consistent with its title—*The Historical Christ*—such a misinterpretation of Jesus' character and personality would have been impossible.

Ignore or misconstrue the facts, and you can turn any historical personality into whatever pleases you. Psychology will never justify or excuse such cavalier reconstructions of reality. The Incarnate God-Man always survives the follies of poor scholarship.

Chapter Three

Snow White, Jung, Obergefell: Archetypal Theology in Action

In my book, *Myth, Allegory, and Gospel*, I briefly described the archetypal psychoanalytic theory of Carl Gustav Jung: for Jung, dreams and fairy-tale imagery reflect fundamental and universal symbols within the human unconscious and can be of immense benefit in analyzing and treating a patient's psychological ills.[1]

In the present essay, we shall employ the virtually universal tale of Snow White. Many readers (including this author) were utterly captivated in childhood by the Disney animated film. The folktale

---

[1] Montgomery, *Myth, Allegory, and Gospel* (Minneapolis: Bethany, 1974).

Figure 1: Snow White; Portrayal by Alexander Zick (1845 - 1907). Unknown date. US work that is in the public domain in the US for an unspecified reason, but presumably because it was published in the US before 1928.

experts Iona and Peter Opie maintain that the story of Snow White can be found with little variation all over the world—"from Ireland to Asia Minor and in several parts of North and West Africa"[2] Let us, therefore, see what psychological, cultural, and theological lessons can be learned from this compelling story.[3]

The Narrative.[4] A queen longs for a child having characteristics shown in a drop of her

---

[2]   Iona and Peter Opie, *The Classic Fairy Tales* (Oxford: Granada, 1980), p. 227.

[3]   Readers may wish to consult the many references to the Snow White story in Jung's *Collected Works*. Valuable also is J. D. Stephen Flynn's essay, "What Fairy Tales Offer the Analysand: A Jungian Exploration of the Fairy Tale Snow White." *Inside Out Journal: Irish Association of Humanistic and Integrative Psychotherapy [IAHIP],* Issue 48 (2006) and later enlargement (2018).

[4]   We recommend as text Maria Tatar (ed.), *The Annotated Brothers Grimm* (New York: W. W. Norton, 2012).

own blood: skin white as snow, hair brilliant black, and ruby-red lips. She gives birth but dies in the process. A year later, the king remarries—to a beautiful but proud and vain woman who reinforces her evil personality traits with a magic mirror telling her that she is "the fairest of all." When Snow White reached seven years of age, the mirror informed her stepmother that her stepdaughter now surpassed her in beauty.

The queen, therefore, instructed a huntsman to take Snow White into a forest and kill her. The huntsman, however, could not bring himself to do this and simply left Snow White alone in the forest. There, she came across a cottage inhabited by seven dwarfs, who took her in and brought her up, teaching her to cook, take care of the house, etc.

The magic mirror revealed to the queen that Snow White still lived, so the queen made attempt after attempt to do away with her by way of a poisoned apple. The fruit, however, put Snow White into a trancelike sleep. The dwarfs, thinking her dead, placed her in a glass coffin to preserve her beauty.

Ultimately, a prince discovered Snow White and fell in love with her, releasing her from her spell. They married with great celebration. The queen, maddened with rage, danced herself to death.

Archetypal meanings. The story focuses on its characters. Let us examine each.

1. *The king.* Hardly described at all, he is, in many ways, the key to understanding the psychology of the tale. The king displays no close personal relationship with his daughter Snow White. He shows no special affection toward her and apparently does nothing himself or through his servants and staff—by instruction or example— to teach her how to live or conduct herself as an adult. Snow White seems to function for her father as little more than window dressing. Jung and many other leading psychoanalytic theorists have stressed the importance of the development in the child of the female (anima) side in the male and the corresponding male (animus) side in the female. Snow White seems to have been left bereft in this respect.

2. *The stepmother.* With her entire interest focused on herself and her willingness even to sacrifice her stepdaughter's life to maintain her status as the "fairest of all," the stepmother represents irredeemable evil. Beauty is no guarantee of moral goodness.

3. *The woodsman.* He is of little importance to the plot, but, though doubtless chosen by the stepmother because of a history of violence, he cannot bring himself personally to harm Snow White. He offers some evidence to Snow

White that her purity is capable of impacting and restraining evil.

4. *The dwarfs.* Their prominence in the Disney version has been criticized for diverting the audience from the central psychological issue: the conflictual relationship between Snow White and her stepmother. But, in fact, the dwarfs comprise a kind of corporate father figure, providing Snow White with the *animus* perspective she never had with her own father, the king, and thus laid the essential foundation for her growth and passage to adulthood. Combining the special characteristic or trait of each dwarf may be seen as modeling a whole person as an ideal.

5. *Snow White.* All commentators have seen her as the epitome of purity, impacted by conditions and forces beyond her understanding or control, but open to grace arriving from outside herself.

6. *The prince.* A transcendent figure, who brings everything to a positive conclusion where all (except the stepmother who refuses to face reality) can "live happily ever after." Snow White can relate to her prince as an *animus* figure, having matured through her psychic development with the dwarfs serving as pseudo-parents.

Finally, a word about the forest environment where Snow White chanced upon the dwarfs. As archetype, the forest represents the nature of our world: mysterious, unfathomable, where the best and the worst can occur. It lacks the security of a castle but is infinitely more open to development and mature growth.

THE WARTBURG

Fascinatingly, Martin Luther's Wartburg experience strongly parallels the forest-and-castle accounts in archetypal fairy tale literature: Luther, at the peril of his life, takes his heroic stand for the Gospel and the Scriptures before Holy Roman Emperor Charles V at Worms. At his Elector's orders, he is mysteriously spirited away to safety in the Wartburg Castle, deep in the Thuringian Forest. He remains there for many months, translating the New Testament "so that every ploughboy can hear God's word." To apply J. R. R. Tolkien's charac-terization of the original Gospel story: "Myth and history have met and fused. God has become the Lord of angels and of men—and of elves."[5]

Figure 2. Luther's desk at Wartburg where he translated the New Testament into German.

Theological understanding. Among the archetypes of redemption, one finds not only Le Père Noël/Santa Claus and his elves (agents of free grace who create and bestow gifts on childlike believers in him, but especially the transcendent Prince—who,

---

[5] Tolkien, "On Fairy Stories." Cf. Montgomery, *op. cit.* (in note 1, above).

as in the Snow White story—appears out of nowhere, seemingly finds the comatose maiden by chance, and through his love for her raises her up to life again.

Snow White theologically represents the human race, deceived and attacked by personal evil power (the devil/Satan), fallen into a deathlike state,[6] but redeemable through the loving, redemptive work of a Messianic Savior.[7]

Legal application: Obergefell. One of the most important U. S. Supreme Court cases in recent years is *Obergefell* prohibiting any American jurisdiction from disallowing same-sex marriage.[8] The arguments for the majority are hopelessly weak against Chief Justice Roberts' detailed and superb dissent, but even that dissent does not touch upon what is surely the most fundamental flaw in same-sex marriage, namely, the absence of *both male and female role models for the children of same-sex unions.* Boys need the presence of the female *anima*; girls (even the most attractive ones, such as Snow White)

---

[6] "Of the tree of the knowledge of good and evil, thou shalt not eat of it: for in the day that thou eatest thereof thou shalt surely die" (Genesis. 2:17); "The wages of sin is death" (Romans 6:23).

[7] Cf. Marie Louise Von Franz, *Redemption Motifs in Fairytales* (Toronto: Inner City Books, 1980).

[8] *Obergefell v Hodges,* 772 F. 3d 388 (decided 26 June 2015).

need serious and continuing contact with the male *animus*. Otherwise, immaturity in the population is virtually guaranteed.

Heterosexual marriage is thus a *sine qua non* for any healthy society. It is utterly naïve to expect seven dwarfs—or their equivalent—to appear by magic to rectify society's stupidities. Thank God (literally) that the redemptive work of Christ as loving Prince Charming is still available for all those not too vain and proud to receive it.

Chapter Four

Human Nature
and Christ's Nature

The tension between Christian psychotherapy
and secular psychoanalysis originated in Sigmund
Freud's conviction that religion is but a pseudo-
solution to psychological problems, and (as an
atheist) that God is an illusion. In spite of hercu-
lean efforts by Christian therapists to counter this
prejudice, which takes no account of the powerful
scientific evidence for the existence of God and
the solid historical evidence for the life, atoning
death, and resurrection of His Son Jesus Christ,[1]

---

[1] See this author's numerous apologetical works, especially
those published by New Reformation Publications and by the
Verlag für Kultur und Wissenschaft, Bonn, Germany (and available in the U.S. from Wipf and Stock).

there is still widespread belief among both believing and unbelieving professionals in the psychological field that the biblical view of human nature is simply incompatible with a psychoanalytic perspective.

Without placing our *imprimatur* on the whole Freudian corpus,[2] we disagree. Freudian analysis has been of inestimable therapeutic aid to sufferers and has beneficially impacted wide areas of contemporary thought. We, therefore, intend in this short essay to demonstrate the compatibility of some of the most fundamental Christian and psychoanalytic factors in the understanding of human nature.

We begin, biblically, with mankind before the fall.

---

[2] We agree with much of the criticism set forth by Richard Webster in his book, *Why Freud Was Wrong: Sin, Science, and Psychoanalysis* (London: HarperCollins, 1995), especially in Part Two ("The Church and the Psychoanalytic Gospel"), pp. 299-510.

Mankind before Sin

Humanity (whatever its physical appearance) was created sinless. That state included the following minimal characteristics: Self-consciousness; Free will; the Id; Rationality; God consciousness; fundamental Morality; Archetypes; Immortality/ eternal life. Unconscious and conscious were in perfect harmony.

Some of these elements need no explanation; others do.

Free will must be understood as entirely *uncaused.* To ask for the "cause" of an act of free will is to pose a nonsense question. This is very important when one treats the fall of mankind into sin. God did not cause this and is therefore not responsible for its deleterious consequences. The Serpent (Satan) did not cause it either but was the agent tempting our first parents to disregard the command of God.

The Freudian *Id* is often misunderstood as a negative drive founded in the selfish pursuit of pleasure, especially along sexual lines (the *libido*); some of Freud's own writing contributed to this unfortunate understanding.[3] In fact, the *Id* refers simply to personal "drives" in general: the fact that all human beings make decisions to act in certain ways rather than otherwise (e.g., to eat now rather than to sleep).[4] The *Id* had no need for the restraints

---

[3] Ruth L. Munroe's *Schools of Psychoanalytic Thought* (New York: Henry Holt, 1955) remains one of the very best sources for understanding the nature and development of Freudian and post-Freudian anthropological ideas.

[4] Cf. Legal philosopher Alan Gewirth's human rights argument that everyone must be accorded *freedom* and *well-being,* i.e., the right to make decisions and the wherewithal to put these decisions into practice. See Montgomery, *Human Rights and Human Dignity* (rev. ed.; Irvine, CA: NRP Books, 2019), pp. 96-98.

of the *Ego* before the fall, since our first parents'
drives were *per se* in line with the divine will. If,
then, the Ego and the Superego were present at the
initial creation of man, their functions lay dormant
until sin entered the picture.

God-consciousness and *fundamental morality*
are declared in Romans 1 to characterize the human
person, and have been present as defining elements
since the beginning of the human race.

Archetypes. What Carl Gustav Jung discovered and described as fundamental imagery at the
root of the human person clearly existed from
the very creation of the race. These archetypes
precede environmental influences, and indeed
function as interpreters of and respondents to
the questions raised by environment. Adam and
Eve would therefore have benefited from them,
though they would not have known negative
archetypes (e.g., figures of the demonic which,
aside from Satan in the neutral form of a serpent,
did not enter Eden).

**The most catastrophic event in human his-
tory was the fall of man from perfection into sin.
The major failing of secular psychoanalytic theory and practice is the denial of the corruption
now at the heart of the human condition. And**

the denial of a cause is inevitably accompanied by a denial of its proper remedy—in this case, the need for divine redemption as the sole satisfactory solution to the root problem of human depravity. Without this perspective, therapies, even when helpful, never arrive at the deepest, underlying level of the human problem.

Mankind after the Fall (from the moment of conception)

Still present are all of the pre-Fall characteristics *except* Immortality/eternal life. To these are added: Self-centeredness; the *Ego* (adjustment of Id demands to reality); Conscience (the *Superego*); Mortality. The unconscious is disengaged from the conscious, so as to become a repository of repressed desires and unwelcome memories.

Noteworthy is the fact that, after the fall, there was no disappearance of rationality (Adam hears, understands, and responds to God's query, "Adam, where are you?"). This contradicts the epistemological presuppositionalism that maintains the impossibility of any effective apologetics argument to unbelievers in a fallen world.

As noted above in our comment on the *Id,* the *Ego* and the *Superego* may have existed prior to The Fall in a dormant state. With the centrality of self-centeredness in fallen man, the *Ego* becomes vital for the adjustment of drives to societal demands and to the external environment; otherwise, people would destroy each other in maximizing each individual's personal desires and goals with no regard for others or the external world. The *Superego* (conscience) is no longer simply the will of God implanted in the human soul but an amalgam of divine standards with human morality (a "morality" generally contaminated by the sinful interests of the individual and his or her societal values). Note that, because of sin, fundamental Morality now requires special revelation (the Bible) to correct self-centered ignoring and misunderstanding of implanted fundamental Morality.

The "Second Adam": Jesus Christ

The Incarnation produced the God-Man, possessed of both divine and human characteristics.

All the divine characteristics are manifest, such as perfect love, but omnipotence, omniscience, and omnipresence are evident only after Christ's resurrection and/or return to the Father in heaven. At the incarnation, together with these divine qualities, our Lord received all the human characteristics possessed by Adam before the Fall, including the perfect harmony of the conscious and the unconscious, plus the post-fall Ego and Mortality). The divine characteristics trump/take precedence over the human characteristics by way of the *communicatio idiomatum*).

Therapeutic Implications

Assuming that the preceding analysis runs true both to Holy Scripture and to psychoanalytic theory, how should the practitioner proceed in the therapeutic context?

The patient must undergo a full and complete physical examination so as to eliminate or correlate with physiological and/or spiritual explanations of his or her condition—never forgetting that multiple sources of the problem may be present.[5] In general,

---

[5] For example, in the case of psychosomatic disorders (somatization; vertigo, tinnitus, sexual and eating difficulties, anorexia and bulimia nervosa, obesity, etc.).

a proper, comprehensive analysis must include the following three levels of examination:

1. Theological/Spiritual[6]
2. Psychological/Psychiatric/Psychoanalytic
3. Physiological/Medical

The therapist must follow the best analytic procedures (classic Freudian and Jungian approaches are especially recommended), omitting, however, any methodologies that contradict biblical teaching or sound doctrine derived from scriptural revelation.

Hypnosis must not be considered "unspiritual." It can open the doors to the unconscious, thereby offering a route to deal with memories, especially repressed early ones, that may lie at the root of the patient's miseries.

The therapist must not avoid issues of sin and redemption.[7] Therefore, questions such as the

---

[6] In our fallen world, this may also embrace the occult/demonic. See Montgomery, *Principalities and Powers: The World of the Occult* (Irvine, CA: New Reformation Publications, 2017). and Montgomery (ed.), *Demon Possession* (2nd ed.; Irvine, CA: NRP Books, 2015).

[7] Cf. Earl D. Bland and Brad D. Strawm (eds.), *Christianity & Psychoanalysis: A New Conversation* (Downers Grove, IL: IVP Academic, 2014), p. 248.

following are vital, even though they may fly in the face of political correctness:

—Do you feel guilt about what has happened/ what you yourself have done?

—How do you think guilt can be removed?

—Have you asked for forgiveness from those you have hurt?

—Have you made proper restitution?

—Do you pray regularly/read the Bible regularly/attend church regularly?

—Have you discussed your problem with your pastor?

—Do you understand/believe the Christian gospel?

—If not, are you open to examining the evidence for it?

—If so, have you asked God in Christ to forgive you?

—Would you pray with me now?

Chapter Five

Marital Problems:
A Psychoanalytic Case
and Analysis

The facts. Mrs. W, 46 years of age, a very successful elementary school teacher, is facing a divorce. She had been married and divorced once before and later had a relationship that did not lead to marriage. Some five years before seeking psychoanalytic help, she married a strong Christian believer. Now that marriage appears to be ending. Her (German) husband claims that she makes married life impossible by frequently flying off the handle, yelling at him, and arbitrarily traveling home (to Portugal) where she can renew contact with former girlfriends. She claims that her husband will not converse sufficiently with her and that she is suffocating at home.

Analytic discoveries. Mrs. W was subjected to incestuous treatment by her father and an older brother during her childhood. She never reported this to authorities out of feelings of guilt. Ultimately, she became a serious Christian and, knowing that she had been forgiven by God through Christ's death on the cross for any wrongdoing on her own part, she ultimately forgave in her own mind both father and brother.

She is a "people person," loving small talk and requiring close and constant contact with girl-friends. However, her husband, as an accountant, prefers professional, more objective conversation and has often become incommunicado with her. In reaction, she suddenly and with no warning left her husband for Portugal, providing no date to return to Germany. Her husband, convinced that this could occur again at any time, has filed for divorce on the grounds of abandonment.

Psychoanalytic understanding and treatment. Mrs. W has evidenced a social preference for her female friends rather than for her husband. Though she claims to be opposed to contemporary philosophies of "woman's liberation," she acts as if she were still single and does not need to even notify her husband as to what she plans to do (such as returning to Portugal)—much less, despite being a Christian believer, allowing him to make final decisions as head of the house. She might well be classified as a psychological (though not a sexual) lesbian.

Mrs. W's incestuous experiences as a child surely lie at the root of her adult conduct—though they conflict with her present beliefs as a committed Christian. Considerable research has shown that those who have suffered incestuously as children very often, in later life as adults, have above-average marital problems, multiple divorces, etc. Her career as an elementary school teacher put her in contact mostly with males of pre-puberty age, who offered no threat comparable to what she had experienced in her childhood.

Psychologically, the victims of incest identify far better with other women than with the male of the species, and they often put the worst construction on male utterances, such as opinions or advice. It seems that to such women, men (especially those in authoritative roles such as one's husband) become identified with the father or other family member/caretaker who instituted the incestuous experiences of their childhood. Anger and antisocial treatment by such persons can reflect the impossibility of such reactions during the early years when the incest(s) occurred.

Studies have reported significant associations between a history of childhood abuse or neglect and various conduct problems, including those classified as oppositional defiant disorder or conduct disorder. Oppositional defiant disorder is indicated by a frequent or persistent pattern of angry or irritable mood, argumentative or defiant behavior, and vindictiveness (APA, 2013a). Its symptoms usually appear during early childhood, often preceding conduct disorder, anxiety disorders, or major depressive disorder. Conduct disorder is indicated by a repetitive or persistent pattern of behavior that violates the basic rights of others or major societal norms or rules, including aggression toward people or animals, destruction of property, deceitfulness or theft, and serious violations of rules (APA, 2013a).

Hostile attributional bias refers to the tendency to assume that someone intended harm when circumstances were ambiguous but a negative outcome was experienced. For example, if a peer spilled milk on a child, the child could assume that the action was benign (unintentional) or intentional, with the latter representing a hostile attributional bias. When children assume that such an action was intentional, they are likely to act aggressively in response (Dodge et al., 1995). Physically abused children are more likely than other children to show such attributional biases (Dodge et al., 1995).... Such biases can lead to a self-fulfilling prophecy whereby children anticipate that someone intends them harm and react in a hostile way, which then elicits a hostile response (Dodge et al., 1995)....

Children who experience abuse or neglect have been found to be at higher risk for the development of externalizing behavior problems, including oppositional defiant disorder, conduct disorder, and aggressive behaviors. Abused and neglected children also have been found to be at increased risk for internalizing problems, particularly depression, in childhood, adolescence, and adulthood.[1]

What is the best therapeutic approach with such a patient? The therapist may employ hypnotic suggestion to recall undesirable childhood events that lie at the root of the current unfortunate personality manifestations. In any event, it is essential

---

[1] *New Directions in Child Abuse and Neglect Research*, ed. Monica Felt, Joshua Joseph, and Anne Petersen (National Research Council, Committee on Child Maltreatment), National Academies Press, 2014, chap. 4.

to assist the patient in seeing that her preference for female relationships is poisoning her marriage and would have that same effect on any future marital situation. She also needs to see that anger in the face of not getting her way cannot be other than non-productive.

In the context of the patient's Christian belief in the institution of marriage, she should be helped to see that a marital union cannot be "democratic" in the sense of limiting action to total agreement or majority vote. After all, only two people are voting, and when there is unresolvable disagreement, only one view can prevail. In biblical terms, such situations require that the husband's view, unless unreasonable and/or immoral, should prevail. To be sure, such instances should be limiting cases, occurring only rarely. The norm is joint agreement, normally the result of prayerful compromise by both parties.

Key therapeutic questions:

(1) Do you think that incest in childhood can have continuing effects in adult life?
(2) Why do you prefer female communication to communication with your husband?
(3) Would your husband agree with your evaluation of his personality? If not, why not?

(4) Do you believe it legitimate that marital deci-
     sions be made unilaterally?
(5) What do you believe the Bible teaches as to the
     locus of authority in a marriage?

N.B. Because of the obvious dangers of coun-
tertransference, it would be preferable that a female,
rather than a male, therapist treat such a patient as
Mrs. W.

Chapter Six

Similitude:
A Proposed Technique
in Psychoanalytic Therapy

Introduction and Abstract

One of the frustrations of psychoanalytic treatment arises when the patient cannot recall his
or her dream life or early childhood memories.
Hypnotherapy offers a possible solution, but, not
uncommonly, the patient refuses hypnosis out
of fear. When these avenues are closed, how can
access to the unconscious be found? We suggest
the employment of what may be termed "similitude
therapy."

Definition

Similitude therapy consists of assisting the patient to recall events in his or her past that parallel events currently taking place. Common examples would include: problems in a previous marriage combined with the death of the previous spouse, leading to difficulties in the current marital relationship; or bad experiences in a previous job when the patient is now in great psychological difficulty in his or her present work situation. The recall of the details of the earlier misery can lead to an awareness of unconscious factors, which, in turn, have direct applicability to the current crisis.

Example[1]

Patient A's life turned around on the sudden death of his first wife. He soon remarried, but now he is constantly plagued by thoughts of how poorly he treated the deceased wife. He is convinced that, whatever he does, it is not sufficient to sustain the right kind of marriage with his present wife, and he

---

[1]   An actual case, but with modification of some factual data to preserve the anonymity of the patient.

frequently breaks into tears and cannot carry out his professional activity as a social worker because of his longing somehow to correct his neglect of his first wife. He imagines his first marriage in idealistic terms and believes that he will inevitably destroy his current union.

Patient A has recently had a complete physical examination and is in good health. He is 52 years of age, without children, and exhibits no neurotic characteristics.

He claims that he does not dream, and, though this is of course not the case, he cannot offer the therapist this avenue into his unconscious. He refuses hypnosis. He has a vague recollection of his childhood relationships with his parents and parent-surrogates (he lived most of his early childhood with his paternal grandmother who was very much occupied with her practice as an accountant, and he had little contact with his father and mother's household, owing to the fact that as a child he suffered from a variety of allergies and could not tolerate the farm smells on his father's clothes). Result: a dearth of information as to the patient's early childhood and a real problem getting him to reveal the landscape of his unconscious. Such a vacuum not only militates against the search for the underlying causes of the patient's current depression but may also detract from the formation of a positive transference relationship between patient and therapist.[2]

In such a situation, the therapist rightly focused on the details of Patient A's first marriage. What, in fact, was the nature of that relationship?

A number of analytic sessions revealed that the deceased wife of Patient A, a retired artist, helped him considerably in the early years of their marriage but, owing to declining health, was unable to do much in the decade preceding her death. Patient A resented this greatly and recriminated against the wife; he may actually have physically abused her.

On the basis of these data, the therapist was in a position to help his patient analyze his personal understanding of the current marriage against the background of the prior union. It became more and more clear that in the current marriage Patient A needed and expected help from his new wife but did not dare request it for fear that it would not be forthcoming or satisfactory—and that, as a consequence, he would begin to treat his present wife

---

[2] See Jean-Claude Filloux, *L'Inconscient* («Que sais-je? » 285; Paris: Presses Universitaires de France, 1970).

as poorly as he had treated his deceased spouse. Furthermore, through this similitude analysis, Patient A discovered that, unconsciously, he had always treated his career as so paramount to all else in his life that he allowed it severely to hurt his personal relationships, particularly those with his spouse. Indeed, the patient became aware of a powerful egoistic factor: that his own career success had been more important to him than his relationship with his spouse(s).

The closer the therapist was able to correlate the data of the two marriages, the more the *similitude* revealed what was occurring in the patient's unconscious. Once the patient realized that he need not and must not make the same demands on his present wife as he had made or expected to be fulfilled in his previous relationship, the less he came unrealistically to idealize the past union. He, therefore, found himself no longer thinking that he was doomed to repeat his mistakes.

As far as Patient A's perhaps justifiable guilt feelings, he was aided by a strong personal Christian belief. He was therefore able to be reminded, through sensitive therapeutic interchange, that redemption and the forgiveness of sins have been achieved by Christ by way of His death on the cross and that, therefore, no additional expiations on the human side were either appropriate or useful.[3]

Conclusion

Underlying the argument of this brief essay is the principle that where normal avenues to the unconscious seem blocked, analogous activity in the patient's past may constitute a vehicle to access the unconscious. The *similitude* between past and present contexts can be employed to break open the seemingly sealed container of the unconscious, thereby opening doors and freeing the therapeutic experience to move forward.

---

[3]   Cf. W. Earl Biddle, *Integration of Religion and Psychiatry* (New York: Collier Books, 1962).

Chapter Seven

Critical Observations On Two Widely Used Introductory Textbooks in Psychoanalytic Psychotherapy

Nancy McWilliams, PSYCHOANALYTIC DIAGNOSIS (2nd Edition; New York and London: Guilford Press, 2020)

McWilliams' book has received high praise from reviewers. Example (for the first edition): "The author fully meets the task she sets out to accomplish using her experiences both as therapist and patient … For those entering the field, it is a must-have text, and for seasoned practitioners, it offers much food for thought" (*The Journal of Nervous and Mental Disease,* 20/03/2004). To such praise should be added the special value of the book: its citation throughout of the important, previously published psychoanalytic literature.

Epistemological Difficulty

McWilliams expresses, both in her Preface/ Introduction and at various points throughout her book, its practical, diagnostic orientation and her lack of focus on "conceptual and philo- sophical problems." In this connection, she seems to equate philosophical analysis with a positivist orientation.

It cannot be too strongly emphasized at the outset that her survey of the diagnostic aspects of the psychoanalytic discipline has been highly praised by virtually every reviewer of her book (see example at the opening of this chapter).

However, philosophical perspective is by no means limited to a naïve positivism along the lines of the Vienna Circle, nor is it incompatible with comprehensive therapeutic analysis. McWilliams' book would have gained much had it benefited from an in-depth discussion of the philosophical issues raised by the diagnostic analyses in the field. Specifically, without any loss of diagnostic content, philosophical discussions of the kind making up Ruth Munroe's classic *Schools of Psychoanalytic Thought*[1] could have been incorporated. This would have immensely strengthened McWilliams' exceedingly brief and simplistic presentation of Freud's views and her far too superficial surveys of a number of other psychoanalytic approaches (Jung, for example).

One of the major problems in the psychoanalytic field is the absence of concern with verification. Theories, such as the Freudian Ego and Id conceptualizations, are offered without any apparent means of establishing their reality. Are such concepts perhaps little more than questionable reifications? Wittgensteinian analytical philosophy has revolutionized the evaluation of traditional metaphysical systems by insisting on solid evidence to support what is often pure speculation. Psychoanalytical diagnosis would surely acquire similar benefits if practitioners were to employ parallel rigor in their analyses.

---

[1] Ruth L. Munroe, *Schools of Psychoanalytic Thought* (New York: Henry Holt, 1955).

Semantic Problem

The logical fallacy of "word magic" has often cleared the air in the sciences as well as in the humanities. Consider, for example, "explanations" that, in reality, are little more than semantic labeling. "Why do the swallows return to San Juan Capistrano at roughly the same time each year?" "Why do the storks return from northern Africa to the Alsace at about the same date each year?" Answer: *Instinct.* What has this answer told us? Precisely nothing since it merely gives a new name to the mysterious phenomenon. "Why do inexplicable biological changes occur evolutionally? Answer: *Mutation.* Again: no explanation at all; merely a new word for the mystery.

There is a particular tendency to commit this fallacy in the professions such as medicine, law, and computing. To a certain extent, the technical lingo as word magic serves as a protective measure, giving the impression to the layman that he or she can never understand the intricacies of the professional's knowledge base.

Employment of such in-group word magic has been a source of immense difficulty in the psychoanalytic realm. That the textbook under discussion is not free of such difficulties is especially evident in the chapters in Part I setting forth primary and secondary defense processes. Such concepts need to be articulated in lay terms and be shown to have concrete and general application beyond the therapeutic. Otherwise, they can become a language of priestcraft, serving largely to wall psychoanalysis off from well-deserved criticism.

II. Matthias Elzer and Alf Gerlach, eds, PSYCHOANALYTIC PSYCHOTHERAPY: A HANDBOOK ("The EFPP Monograph Series"; London: Routledge, 2018

This textbook has been lauded by its reviewers. A typical example is the evaluation by Anne-Marie Sandler, past president of the British Psychoanalytic Society and of the European Psychoanalytic Association: "An excellent and well-presented overview.… This lucid, detailed, and well-written book is the result of years of teaching and will appeal to all the workers in the therapeutic field and many others interested in psychoanalytic therapy."

In its Preface, the editors note that the book is a compilation of materials by a number of contributors in the field and that, therefore, there may be overlaps and duplications within the published work. There are also, inevitably, different levels of depth in the ten chapters. But the result, though not homogeneous, is an excellent practical introduction to the psychoanalytic field.

The Germanic orientation of the book seems to us to be an advantage, not a disadvantage. Academic and professional disciplines, including psychotherapy, tend toward ingrownness, particularly in the Western hemisphere and in the English-speaking world. A broader, more international perspective can only enhance the study of the subject.

Our sole problem with the book is the absence of an area of analysis that we believe is of great importance but neglected in virtually all of the professional literature introducing psychotherapy to students. The same point applies to our evaluation of McWilliams' *Psychoanalytic Diagnosis* (supra).

A general textbook in any academic discipline cannot be expected to include everything. The more complex the field, the more latitude should be granted to the author to restrict coverage to the most essential areas. Elzer and Gerlach's book does an impressive job of covering most therapeutic areas and concerns.

However, one vital area, embracing both psychoanalytic practice and theory, is entirely neglected: the patient's religious orientation and worldview. We learn nothing about how religious belief impacts the psychic health or illness of the patient. Since one's fundamental beliefs impact one's manner of understanding and coping with others and the external world, they can be ignored only at the therapist's peril.

It is hardly a justification for this omission to argue that the revealing of the therapist's own religious position can result in dangerous coun-tertransference.[2] There could surely have been a chapter, or a section of a chapter, devoted to the kind of scholarly analysis included in, for example, Knabb *et al., Christian Psychotherapy in Context.*[3] Elzer and Gerlach's book is composite, involving a number of contributors; therefore, adding the

---

[2] Cf. N. A. Moukaddam, et al., "Instant countertransference affects assessment and treatment recommendations for depression in patients openly professing religious faith," 6/2 Spirituality in Clinical Practice [American Psychological Association/ APA PsychNet], 100-109 (June, 2019). Cf. Earl D. Bland and Brad D. Strawm (eds.), *Christianity & Psychoanalysis: A New Conversation* (Downers Grove, IL: IVP Academic, 2014), p. 248.

[3] J. J. Knabb, et al., *Christian Psychotherapy in Context: Theoretical and Empirical Explorations in Faith-Based Mental Health* (London: Routledge, 2019).

religious dimension would not have altered its fundamental framework.

The most basic religious issue requiring attention is the nature of the patient's personal religious conviction: is it of an *objective* or a *subjective* nature?—i.e., does it derive from an external, revelatory source, or is it the product of the patient's own religious experience and/or sociological orientation?[4].

Here the key distinction is between Christian belief, regardless of denomination, and virtually all other religions. Christian believers derive their position from biblical revelation and/or church doctrine, whereas non-Christian religions rely upon personal or sociological experience for their religious perspective.[5] To be sure, there are "middle of the road" church people whose belief structure pays little attention to the Bible, but when dealing with a self-confessed Christian, the therapist must endeavor to determine how the

---

[4]   See J. W. Montgomery, "Constructive Religious Empiricism: An Analysis and Criticism," in his *The Shape of the Past* (Minneapolis: Bethany, 1975), pp. 257-311.

[5]   One might think that Islamic belief is essentially of the revelatory variety, but Qur'anic faith is almost entirely walled off from the objective (Muhammad's "miraculous night journey" occurred so rapidly that there were no witnesses to it).

patient's values relate to his or her revelational understanding.

And what about the "unbelievers" or the "atheists"? Here, it is vital to understand that these positions are, in fact, religious since they deal with what Paul Tillich and others have deemed "ultimate concerns."[6] "L'atheisme peut encore être l'equivalent d'une croyance particuliere."[7] That is to say, the "non-believer" does, in fact, believe in "something," even though he or she may frame it in negative terms. The therapist will need to get to the root of this belief system, no less than in the more usual case of a professed believer.

The issue of *guilt* often arises in religious contexts. Here there is the frequently encountered phenomenon of irrational reductionism on the therapist's part—an attempt to dismiss "sin" as a mere aberration of the troubled patient. As an undergraduate at Cornell, I met more than one returning serviceman from the battlefields of World War II who said that they were not sure

---

[6] Cf. Marie-Jean Sauret, ´Freud, le juif athee," *Freud et l'inconscient* ("Les Essentiels Milan"; Liguge, France: Aubin, 2002), pp. 50-53.

[7] Pierre Marchais, *Magie et mythe en psychiatrie* (Paris; Masson, 1977), p. 183.

of God's existence, but they had no doubts about the devil's.

For the Christian believer, the question is often whether the patient really believes that Christ's death on the cross and resurrection from the dead cancels out the penalty of sin or whether the patient must still try to achieve this through his or her own efforts (good works, etc.). The central doctrine of the Protestant Reformation, justification by grace alone, through faith alone, should keep such patients from playing the hopeless game of constructing towers of Babel by which one can supposedly reach heaven through one's own inherent goodness.

Depth analysis of the patient's religious situation may thus open doors to the sources of neurosis and psychosis that would otherwise go unobserved and, therefore, inadequately or superficially treated.

Appendix: Sample Therapist's Questions to Patient A

What adult did you most enjoy being with during your childhood?

Why did you live with your grandmother and not with your parents?

Why did you choose social work as a career?

Did you have a close relationship with your first wife?

Did that relationship change in the course of the marriage? If so, why do you think that happened?

Did you grieve immediately on the death of your first wife? If not, when did the grieving begin?

Did your first wife assist you in your career activities?

How soon after the death of your first wife did you remarry?

Does your present wife assist you in your career activities?

Why do you think your grief for your first wife's death suggests problems with your second marriage?

Would you consider yourself a religious person? If so, how do you understand God's forgiveness?

What do you imagine your reactions to be should your present wife pass away?

How important is your career to you?

Chapter Eight

Basic Rules for Successful Christian Psychoanalysis

1. Therapeutic focus must not be anthropocentric but Christocentric; not merely on what heals but on what saves.
2. The archetypal serpent can be a transitional symbol—from the Tempter in Eden to the Serpent in the Wilderness.
3. Analysis can succeed only when both transference and countertransference are given their full weight.
4. As in cooking, the time factor is critical.
5. Analysis cannot succeed unless the patient dies and is resurrected.
6. Adjustment to the perspective of one's family, colleagues, or associates achieves nothing per se; all depends on the nature of that perspective

and the extent to which it conjoins with the patient's deepest needs.

7. As the therapeutic process comes to a close, the analyst must ask himself or herself not only whether the illness (neurosis, psychosis, etc.) for which the patient sought help has been successfully treated or at least brought under adequate social control *but also* (since psychological wholeness entails nothing less than a right relationship with God, one's neighbor, and oneself): Is the patient now more or less Christlike in his or her values, aims, and ideals than when therapy commenced? And the awkward related query: Has the therapist thereby reached a greater level of personal and professional understanding?

Appendix. Medical History Form

NEW PATIENT
MEDICAL HISTORY FORM

Full Name: _____   Date: _____

Birth Date: _____   Age: _____

ALLERGIES   ❏ NO ALLERGIES

ALLERGY	ALLERGIC REACTION

MEDICATIONS

MEDICATIONS (Please list ALL)	DOSE (Mg., pill, etc.)	TIMES PER DAY

If you need more room to list medications, please write them on a blank sheet of paper with the required information

HEALTH MAINTENANCE SCREENING TEST HISTORY

CHOLESTEROL	Date:	Facility/Provider:	Abnormal Result? Y N
COLONOSCOPY/SIGMOID	Date:	Facility/Provider:	Abnormal Result? Y N
MAMMOGRAM	Date:	Facility/Provider:	Abnormal Result? Y N
PAP SMEAR	Date:	Facility/Provider:	Abnormal Result? Y N
BONE DENSITY	Date:	Facility/Provider:	Abnormal Result? Y N

VACCINATION HISTORY

Last Tetanus Booster or TdaP:	Last Pnuemovax *(Pneumonia)*:
Last Flu Vaccine:	Last Prevnar:
Last Zoster Vaccine *(Shingles)*:	

PERSONAL MEDICAL HISTORY

DISEASE/CONDITION	CURRENT	PAST	COMMENTS
Alcoholism/Drug Abuse			
Asthma			
Cancer (type:_____)			
Depression/Anxiety/Bipolar/Suicidal			
Diabetes (type:_____)			
Emphysema (COPD)			
Heart Disease			
High Blood Pressure (hypertension)			
High Cholesterol			
Hypothyroidism/Thyroid Disease			
Renal (kidney) Disease			
Migraine Headaches			
Stroke			
Other:			
Other:			

SURGERIES

TYPE (specify left/right)	DATE	LOCATION/FACILITY

WOMEN'S HEALTH HISTORY

Date of Last Menstrual Cycle:	Age of First Menstruation: _____ Age of Menopause: _____
Total Number of Pregnancies:	Number of Live Births:
Pregnancy Complications:	

Patient Name: _____ DOB: _____

FAMILY MEDICAL HISTORY ❑ NO SIGNIFICANT FAMILY HISTORY IS KNOWN

✔ CHECK ALL THAT APPLY	Alcohol/Drug Abuse	Asthma	Cancer (type: ___)	Emphysema (COPD)	Depression/Anxiety	Bipolar/Suicidal	Diabetes	Early Death	Heart Disease	High Cholesterol	High Blood Pressure	Kidney Disease	Stroke	Thyroid Disease	Migraines	Other:	Other:	Other:
Mother																		
Father																		
Brother																		
Sister																		
Child																		
MGM																		
MGF																		
PGM																		
PGF																		
Other:_____																		

SOCIAL HISTORY

Occupation (or prior occupation):	❑ Retired ❑ Unemployed ❑ LOA ❑ Disabled
Employer:	Years of Education or Highest Degree:
If employed, do you work the night shift? Y N N/A	
Marital Status (check one): ❑ Single ❑ Partner ❑ Married ❑ Divorced ❑ Widowed ❑ Other:_____	
Do you have children? Y N	If yes, how many?

OTHER HEALTH ISSUES

TOBACCO USE	Smoke Cigarettes? Y N (If you never smoked, please move to Alcohol/Drug Use)		
Current: Packs/day ____ # of Years ____	**Past:** Quit Date: _____	Packs/day ____	# of Years ____
Other Tobacco (check one): ❑ Pipe ❑ Cigar ❑ Snuff ❑ Chew			
ALCOHOL/DRUG USE	Do you drink alcohol? Y N	❑ Beer ❑ Wine ❑ Liquor	# of Drinks/week:
Do you use marijuana or recreational drugs? Y N		Have you ever used needles to inject drugs? Y N	
Have you ever taken someone else's drugs? Y N			

Patient Name: _____ DOB: _____

OTHER HEALTH ISSUES continued...

SEXUAL ACTIVITY	Sexually involved currently? Y N *(If no sexual history, please continue to Exercise)*		
Sexual partner(s) is/are/have been: ❑ Male ❑ Female			
Birth control method: ❑ None ❑ Condom ❑ Pill/Ring/Patch/Inj/IUD ❑ Vasectomy			
EXERCISE	Do you exercise regularly? Y N *(If you answered no, please move to Sleep)*		
What kind of exercise?		**Duration:** How long (min.): _____ How often: _____	
SLEEP	How many hours, on average, do you sleep at night *(or during the day, if working night shift)*?		
DIET	How would you rate your diet? ❑ Good ❑ Fair ❑ Poor	Would you like advice on your diet? Y N	
SAFETY	Do you use a bike helmet? Y N	Do you use seat belts consistently? Y N	
Working smoke detector in home? Y N		If you have guns at home, are they locked up? Y N	
Is violence at home a concern for you? Y N		Have you completed an Advance Directive for Health Care (ADHC), Living Will, or Physical Orders for Life Sustaining Therapy (POLST)? Y N	

OTHER PROVIDERS/SPECIALISTS

SPECIALIST	NAME	LAST VISIT
Cardiology		
Gastroenterologist (GI)		
OB/GYN		
Neurology		
Pulmonary		
Other:_____		
Other:_____		

ADDITIONAL INFORMATION

Have you traveled outside of the country in the last 30 days? Y N	If yes, where?
Have you served in the military? Y N	If yes, how long and what branch?
Were you deployed? Y N	If yes, where?

Patient Name: _____   DOB: _____

REVIEW OF SYSTEMS ✔ CHECK ALL THAT APPLY

CONSTITUTION	CARDIOVASCULAR	SKIN
Activity change	Chest pain	Color change
Appetite change	Leg swelling	Pallor
Chills	Palpitations	Rash
Diaphoresis	**GASTROINTESTINAL**	Wound
Fatigue	Abdominal distention	**ALLERGY/IMMUNO**
Fever	Abdominal pain	Environmental allergies
Unexpected weight change	Anal bleeding	Food allergies
HEAD, EAR, NOSE & THROAT	Blood in stool	Immunocompromised
Congestion	Constipation	**NEUROLOGICAL**
Dental problem	Diarrhea	Dizziness
Drooling	Nausea	Facial asymmetry
Ear discharge	Rectal pain	Headaches
Ear pain	Vomiting	Light-headedness
Facial swelling	**ENDOCRINE**	Numbness
Hearing loss	Cold intolerance	Seizures
Mouth sores	Heat intolerance	Speech difficulty
Nosebleeds	Polydipsia	Syncope
Postnasal drip	Polyphagia	Tremors
Rhinorrhea	Polyuria	Weakness
Sinus pressure	**GENITOURINARY**	**HEMATOLOGIC**
Sneezing	Difficulty urinating	Adenopathy
Sore throat	Dysuria	Bruises/bleeds easily
Tinnitus	Enuresis	**PSYCHIATRIC**
Trouble swallowing	Flank pain	Agitation
Voice change	Frequency	Behavior problem
EYES	Genital sore	Confusion
Eye discharge	Hematuria	Decreased concentration
Eye itching	Penile discharge	Dysphoric mood
Eye pain	Penile pain	Hallucinations
Eye redness	Penile swelling	Hyperactive
Photophobia	Scrotal swelling	Nervous/anxious
Visual disturbance	Testicular pain	Self-injury
RESPIRATORY	Urgency	Sleep disturbance
Apnea	Urine decreased	Suicidal ideas
Chest tightness	**MUSCULAR**	
Choking	Arthralgias	
Cough	Back pain	
Shortness of breath	Gait problems	
Stridor	Joint swelling	
Wheezing	Myalgias	
	Neck pain	
	Neck stiffness	

Patient Name: _____   DOB: _____

Appendix: Initial Medical Examination Form [as 6-page attachment]

MEDICAL HISTORY FORM

Date: _____ / _____ / _____

NAME: _____ Birthdate: _____ / _____ / _____

	Last	First	M. I.	
Age:		Sex:	Gender:	Sexual Preference:
Current Weight: _____ Height: _____		Highest Known Weight: _____		Lowest Known Weight: _____

How did you hear about us?   Center?

Describe briefly your present symptoms:

Please list your primary care physician and specialists that you currently see: (include their name & location):

Please list any medical hospitalizations (include where, when, & for what reason):

Please list any psychiatric hospitalizations/partial hospitalization programs/respites (include where, when, & for what reason):

Have you had psychotherapy or are you currently in psychotherapy? (include where, when & therapist's name):

Have you ever struggled with Eating or Body Image? ☐ Yes   ☐ No   If so, please circle all that apply:

Restricting   Binging   Purging   Over Exercise   Chewing and spitting out food

Laxative Use   Food Avoidance   Fear of Certain Foods   Body Checking   Fear of looking at mirror

Readjusting clothes throughout the day   Difficulty leaving the home d/t appearance   Frequent changing cloth

PAST MEDICAL HISTORY

Do you now or have you ever had:

- ❏ Diabetes
- ❏ High blood pressure
- ❏ High cholesterol
- ❏ Hypothyroidism
- ❏ Goiter
- ❏ Cancer (type) _____
- ❏ Leukemia
- ❏ Psoriasis
- ❏ Angina
- ❏ Heart problems

- ❏ Heart murmur
- ❏ Pneumonia
- ❏ Pulmonary embolism
- ❏ Asthma
- ❏ Emphysema
- ❏ Stroke
- ❏ Epilepsy (seizures)
- ❏ Cataracts
- ❏ Kidney disease
- ❏ Kidney stones

- ❏ Crohn's disease
- ❏ Colitis
- ❏ Anemia
- ❏ Jaundice
- ❏ Hepatitis
- ❏ Stomach or peptic ulcer
- ❏ Rheumatic fever
- ❏ Tuberculosis
- ❏ HIV/AIDS

Other medical conditions (please list):

Past Surgical History:

Please list all surgeries, dates and locations:

REPRODUCTIVE/SEXUAL HISTORY:

Females Only:

Age of first period:

Pregnancies:

Miscarriages:

Abortions:

Do you have regular periods?   ❏ Yes ❏ No

Have you reached menopause? ❏ Yes ❏ No At what age?

For Everyone:

Do you struggle with infertility ❏ Yes   ❏ No   If yes, please describe:

Are you currently being treated with hormone replacement therapy? ❏ Yes   ❏ No   If yes, please describe:

Have you ever had Gender Reassignment Surgery (GRS)? ❏ Yes   ❏ No
If yes, please circle: male to female or female to male?

FAMILY HISTORY				
	IF LIVING		**IF DECEASED**	
	Age (s)	Health & Psychiatric	Age(s) at death	Cause
Father				
Mother				
Siblings				
Children				

EXTENDED FAMILY PSYCHIATRIC PROBLEMS PAST & PRESENT:
Maternal Relatives:

Paternal Relatives:

DRUG ALLERGIES
Do you have any drug allergies? ☐ Yes   ☐ No
Please list any drug allergies, reactions and age of onset:

CURRENT MEDICATIONS
Please list any medications that you are now taking. Include non-prescription or over the counter medications & vitamins or supplements:

Name of Drug:	Dose (including how many times per day):	How long have you been taking this?
1.		
2.		
3.		
4.		
5.		
6.		
7.		
8.		
9.		
10.		

PAST PSYCHIATRIC MEDICATIONS
Please list any psychiatric medications that you took in the past.

Name of drug	How long did you take it?	Please list side effects:
1.		
2.		
3.		
4.		
5.		
6.		
7.		
8.		
9.		
10.		

SYSTEMS REVIEW

In the past month, have you had any of the following problems?

GENERAL	NERVOUS SYSTEM	PSYCHIATRIC
❏ Recent weight gain; amount	❏ Headaches	❏ Depression
❏ Recent weight loss: amount___	❏ Dizziness	❏ Excessive worries
❏ Fatigue	❏ Fainting or loss of consciousness	❏ Difficulty falling asleep
❏ Weakness	❏ Numbness or tingling	❏ Difficulty staying asleep
❏ Fever	❏ Memory loss	❏ Difficulties with sexual arousal
		❏ Intrusive thoughts
MUSCLE/JOINTS/BONES	**STOMACH AND INTESTINES**	❏ Frequent crying
❏ Numbness	❏ Nausea	❏ Sensitivity
❏ Joint pain	❏ Heartburn	❏ Thoughts of suicide / attempts
❏ Muscle weakness	❏ Stomach pain	❏ Stress
❏ Joint swelling Where?	❏ Vomiting	❏ Irritability
	❏ Yellow jaundice	❏ Poor concentration
EARS	❏ Increasing constipation	❏ Racing thoughts
❏ Ringing in ears	❏ Persistent diarrhea	❏ Hallucinations
❏ Loss of hearing	❏ Blood in stools	❏ Rapid speech
❏ Pain		❏ Mood swings
❏ Redness	**BLOOD**	❏ Anxiety
❏ Loss of vision	❏ Anemia	❏ Risky behavior
❏ Double or blurred vision	❏ Clots	
❏ Dryness		
	KIDNEY/URINE/BLADDER	**FEMALE ONLY:**
THROAT	❏ Frequent or painful urination	❏ Abnormal Pap smear
❏ Frequent sore throats	❏ Blood in urine	❏ Irregular periods
❏ Hoarseness		❏ Bleeding between periods
❏ Difficulty in swallowing	**SKIN**	❏ PMS
❏ Pain in jaw	❏ Redness	
	❏ Rash	**OTHER PROBLEMS:**
HEART AND LUNGS	❏ Nodules/bumps	
❏ Chest pain	❏ Hair loss	
❏ Palpitations	❏ Color changes of hands or feet	
❏ Shortness of breath		
❏ Fainting		
❏ Swollen legs or feet		
❏ Cough		

PERSONAL HISTORY

Were there problems with your birth? (specify)
Where were your born & raised?

What is your highest education?   ❏High school ❏Some college ❏College graduate ❏Advanced degree

Marital status: ❏ Never married ❏ Married ❏ Divorced ❏ Separated ❏ Widowed ❏ Partnered/significant other
What is your current or past occupation?

Are you currently working? : ❏ Yes ❏ No   Hours/week _____   If not, are you ❏ retired ❏ disabled ❏ sick leave?

Who do you live with?   Do you have any children? ❏ Yes ❏ No Ages?
                                         Do you have any pets? ❏ Yes ❏ No

Have you ever had legal problems? (specify)

Religion:

SUBSTANCE USE

DRUG CATEGORY (circle each substance used)	Age when you first used this:	How much & how often did you use this?	How many years did you use this?	When did you last use this?	Do you currently use this?	
ALCOHOL					Yes ☐	No ☐
CANNABIS: Marijuana, oil, lotion					Yes ☐	No ☐
STIMULANTS: Cocaine, crack					Yes ☐	No ☐
STIMULANTS: Methamphetamine—speed					Yes ☐	No ☐
AMPHETAMINES/OTHER STIMULANTS: Ritalin, Dexedrine					Yes ☐	No ☐
BENZODIAZEPINES/TRANQUILIZERS: Valium, Librium, Halcion, Xanax, Diazepam, Ativan, Klonopin					Yes ☐	No ☐
SEDATIVES/HYPNOTICS/BARBITURATES: Phenobarbital					Yes ☐	No ☐
HEROIN					Yes ☐	No ☐
STREET OR ILLICIT METHADONE					Yes ☐	No ☐
OTHER OPIOIDS: Tylenol #2 & #3, 282'S, 292'S, Percodan, Percocet, Opium, Morphine, Demerol, Dilaudid					Yes ☐	No ☐
HALLUCINOGENS: LSD, PCP, STP, MDA, DAT, mescaline, peyote, mushrooms, ecstasy (MDMA), nitrous oxide					Yes ☐	No ☐
INHALANTS: Glue, gasoline, aerosols, paint thinner					Yes ☐	No ☐
OTHER: (specify) _____ _____ _____					Yes ☐	No ☐

Illustrations

Alsace, showing Kaysersberg near Colmar

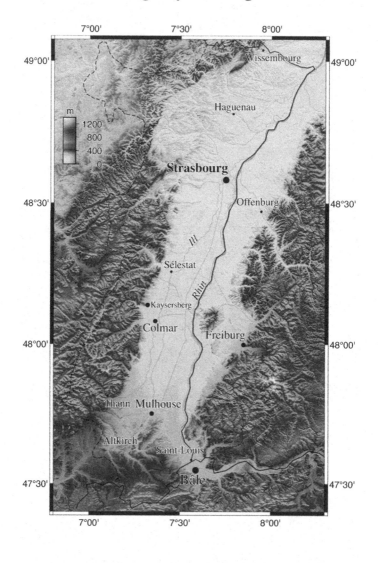

Dr. Montgomery lecturing at the Schweitzer memorial